puzzle therapy

SELF-LOVE

GAMES & ACTIVITIES

125 Word Searches, Mazes, & Games to Boost Your Happiness, Resilience, & Well-Being

ISADORA BAUM

ADAMS MEDIA

New York   London   Toronto   Sydney   New Delhi

T0047152

Adams Media
An Imprint of Simon & Schuster, Inc.
100 Technology Center Drive
Stoughton, Massachusetts 02072

First Adams Media trade paperback edition August 2021

ADAMS MEDIA and colophon are trademarks of Simon & Schuster.

For information about special discounts for bulk purchases, please contact Simon & Schuster Special Sales at 1-866-506-1949 or business@simonandschuster.com.

The Simon & Schuster Speakers Bureau can bring authors to your live event. For more information or to book an event contact the Simon & Schuster Speakers Bureau at 1-866-248-3049 or visit our website at www.simonspeakers.com.

Interior design by Michelle Kelly
Interior images © 123RF/Sviatlana Sheina
Crosswords and word searches by Charles Timmerman
Mazes by Priscilla Yuen
Coloring © 123RF

Manufactured in the United States of America

2 2023

ISBN 978-1-5072-1624-8

Dedication

Self-love grows internally, but external forces can impact the way you see, accept, and appreciate yourself. This book is dedicated to the people in my life who have helped shape my own self-love journey. I have come to understand what love I want to attract, the kind of love I *know* I deserve, and how best I can genuinely share love in return. Whether you have given me a lifelong love or a single lesson—I now have lifelong self-love, for which I am incredibly grateful.

Acknowledgments

I want to thank Adams Media, Simon & Schuster, and all other editors and collaborators with whom I have worked with over the years. I also want to thank my mother, for she has always been my greatest supporter. Thank you for being there for me through the ups and downs—as both a shoulder to cry on and the first to raise a toast. I love you, Mom.

Contents

Introduction

Self-love is the act of showing compassion, kindness, confidence, and adoration to your mind, body, and spirit. It is the most powerful gift you can give yourself: It builds and fosters confidence, bravery, authenticity, and the ability to love others in return.

Let's face it: Life can (and will!) throw obstacles your way—such as breakups, career setbacks, and self-doubt. The beauty of self-love is that it will help you get past the hard times with an upbeat attitude and positive perspective since you believe in yourself and value your self-worth.

In this book, you will find a variety of puzzles, activities, word games, and writing and reflection exercises, as well as positive affirmations and mantras. The 125 exercises will help you combat boredom and keep your mind sharp—and they'll also lead to greater insight into, and development of, your own sense of self. This type of reflection will help you get in tune with your mind, body, and soul to attract the love you deserve in various aspects of your life.

As you journey through this book, you'll gain experience in eliminating toxicity, letting in love and affection, and working toward becoming your best self. You'll also boost self-love through the implementation of daily habits built around self-care, as well as the reevaluation and strengthening of interpersonal relationships, career goals, and more.

Turn these pages to travel the maze to Find Your Flow, brainstorm ways to Pamper Yourself with Special Indulgences, solve the word search to Cultivate Beauty from Within, and more. Let's start showing love to the most unique, wonderful person on Earth—you!

How to Use This Book

You can use this book in any way that works for you. You can jump to a page that resonates with a situation you're experiencing at the moment, or go through page by page and absorb a variety of inspirations. Approach each activity as a fun way to pass the time and challenge your brain—but then take each maze destination, crossword clue, coloring page theme, and word scramble phrase to heart as you strengthen your self-care practice and boost your self-love.

The writing exercises consist of reflection activities, mantras, meditations, and affirmations. These journaling prompts will allow you to discover your truest desires and reevaluate your relationships to make sure you are fostering those that bring about self-love and forgoing toxic elements that may be holding you back from reaching your greatest potential.

Sit down in a quiet space—with a pen, pencil, and markers or colored pencils—and enjoy these exercises with an open mind and heart. Recite the affirmations each morning for a brighter day. Mix and match activities to shake up your self-care routine. Most of these exercises are not one-and-done—you can do many of them again and again for a continual boost in love and acceptance for yourself as you go about your life's ever-changing journey.

GAMES & ACTIVITIES

Cultivate Beauty from Within

As you search for these words, meditate on all the ways you can search for and appreciate the beauty you have within yourself. Pick five of these qualities and create an intention to represent and act on each one today.

ACCEPTING
APPRECIATIVE
BIG HEART
CARING
COMPASSIONATE
EMPATHY
FORGIVING

GENUINE
GOOD PERSON
GRACIOUS
KINDNESS
LOVE
LOYALTY
PLAYFUL

POSITIVE
RESPECT
SUPPORTIVE
TOLERANT
TRUE INTENTIONS
TRUSTWORTHY

```
R S W G S G C Z P N O I A M N E Q J
F H T L U F Y A L P A N Z I O Y P O
W N I Y O O G V Y Q S Y U N S T I X
O Y G N I R A C T C E P S E R L W T
S I Q Z C H Q L E V W N G U E A Q Y
F Z D C A H E O M U Q J E V P Y F D
P V F O R G I V I N G I I N D O G T
P T W M G H U E I Z N T X A O L G R
Y F S P A K A E E T A Z Y P O X Z I
R N O A Q C I T E I R H G H G E P T
T P E S Z R C N C U T O I M G V U F
O G B S U Z T E D A S I P P E I R B
L Z J I L I R S P N R W T P N T V K
E Z J O O P N M V T E D D E U I M H
R A I N P S E D V Y I S K R I S P H
A O S A M H D O V Q Z N S B N O O F
N Y H T R O W T S U R T G G E P B G
T R A E H G I B B D Z U V X F D Q R
```

Love Yourself

As you color, imagine your love for yourself
growing and growing—you have no limits!

Boost Your Confidence

Unscramble these terms, then use the bolded letters to solve the puzzle to reveal something you have inside yourself, all the time, to boost your confidence.

RIAE**SP**   _____

STI**O**VEIP LKAT   _____

AN**A**M**T**R   _____

ISFOFNA**R**AIMT   _____

LF**E**S-OHR**W**T   _____

LO**D**B   _____

DOGO DTIAT**E**UT   _____

VOEL ORYS**FU**LE   _____

TOETDXERR**V**E   _____

LCSOAEIB   _____

— — — — — — — — — — — — — — — — —

Follow Your Heart

When you pursue a romantic connection with another person, you create the opportunity to establish more meaningful connections, which is also an act of self-love. As you search for someone worthy of your love, try to trust your gut as opposed to your head, where you might get tangled up in overanalyzing things.

Begin this maze by focusing on trusting your gut instincts. As you find your way around the maze, you'll see reminders along the way to trust and love yourself. Keep searching until you end up at your heart's desires.

Take Deep Breaths

Breath work calms the body and focuses the mind. Try this simple breathing exercise to refocus and recenter yourself.

- Put a mat down in a dark, calm space. You can lie down on the mat or sit upright with your legs crossed. Focus on observing your breath.

- Inhale for a count of three. Hold your breath for a moment, then release in an exhale for a count of three.

- With each inhale, think of words that represent self-love, such as beauty and kindness.

- Repeat for a total of five to ten minutes.

Empower Yourself

As you search for the answers to fill in this crossword, also look for ways to locate and celebrate the power you have inside you at all times.

Across
1 Lady Gaga song
5 A plant does this
8 Trust your _____
9 "Lose You to Love Me" singer
10 Get back on the _____
11 Sweet green _____ (vegetable)

Down
2 Lizzo lyric: "I am my _____"
3 Love _____ to love others
4 Special
6 Keep going
7 Opposite of failure

Pamper Yourself with Special Indulgences

Treating yourself to a special experience every once in a while is a great way to recharge your body, mind, and spirit. Choose an option from each column to find an activity that will give you what you need right now—whether that's a sense of relaxation or a boost of energy.

Recharge with an invigorating...	glass of wine.
Take deep breaths as you indulge in a...	chocolate bar.
Grab a friend and enjoy a...	bath.
Pamper yourself alone with a...	cup of herbal tea.
Jot down some thoughts about your favorite...	walk in nature.
Notice your five senses as you savor a...	book.
Schedule time to enjoy a...	massage.
Try a new type of...	funny TV show.

Create More Wealth

Are you trying to boost your earning power? The answer might lie in self-care. The fear of not succeeding can stunt growth in general, and wealth and prosperity in particular. Conquer this fear by reminding yourself of all the skills and unlimited potential you have. As a first step, think of ways you could make more money through different ventures—such as taking on a side gig teaching someone a skill and more!

Start in the center of this maze and find your way out through the various options as you visualize yourself manifesting wealth, both material and spiritual.

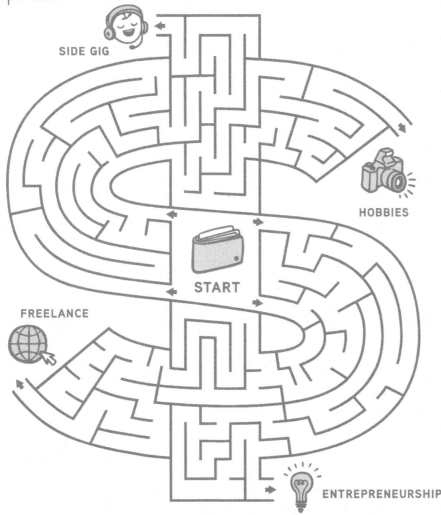

Celebrate Your Gifts

As you color, think of all the gifts you have inside you now,
as well as the gifts you deserve to receive.

Find Your People

Getting rid of toxic relationships in favor of healthy, loving ones is how you'll find your true support system. Allocate your time well—spend quality time and give your heart and effort to those who have your back in return and help you be and feel your best self.

Meditate on who in your life brings you joy and positive energy, and who tends to make you feel uneasy. Ask yourself if there is a way to maximize your positive influences and minimize your negative ones.

Explore Feelings of Touch

Gentle and loving touch is a very important part of a healthy life. Pick five of these ideas to give to yourself, and pick five to give to others.

CARESS
CUDDLE
EMBRACE
GENTLY
HEARTWARMING
HOLD HANDS
HUG

KISS
LATHER
MASSAGE
PAT
PROTECTION
RUB
SNUGGLE

SOOTHING
SPOON
SQUEEZE
STROKE
SUPPORT
TICKLE

```
G D I B D J X T V D J C I O U H M J
W G P T N T D D T G Y J A J D T G Y
K U N F X L X U K G Q T Z V O R N L
P Y W I K M S L V D X V M I G O N C
M U W G M U D S A I G Y O S W P C J
Z S M E T R N O I T C E T O R P L L
N Z K F L P A O H E H J X O U U W J
N W P C X D H W V C I E D T F S O Y
L C Q H G R D E T A E G R H T L G K
S Q U U F E L U H R M L E I C O R T
U G D W U K O F C B A B G N X P L Q
C C P J C I H G M M S E U G T Y R J
G J A I F S R C P E S Q H R U L K A
P Y T Z A S W S A T A O U J Y N Y V
U P R P Y T A P R R G S U E Z P S J
F C S N K S D O F J E M F Y E F X R
F J P B V P K O E T R S L X I Z A Z
I Q N Y T E Y N F A P Z S S I Q E S
```

Remind Yourself
That You're a Fighter

Obstacles come your way; disagreements and conflicts arise. In these times, you may feel frustrated and emotional. You may feel trapped, unable to hold your ground, and then act in ways you regret.

Look in the mirror and say this affirmation:

"I am above this.
I do not fail."

Calm Your Mind

Your mind can get boggled and muddied from the business of everyday life, so periodically take a moment to clear it. The following ideas can promote clarity and relaxation. Take an idea, time, or location from the first column and pair it with a theme from the second column to vary up the ways you reset yourself, and begin again with a clean slate.

Journal	Gratitude
Meditation	Peace
Exercise	Love
Deep Breaths	Sleep
Morning	Yoga
Evening	Reflection
Afternoon	Mindset
Outside	Music

Appreciate the Little Things about Yourself

Write down five things you love about yourself and/or consider your strengths. These should be little attributes or gestures that have made an impact on yourself or on others or that make you feel proud. Alongside each, create an action step to display that quality in the future.

1: _____

2: _____

3: _____

4: _____

5: _____

Focus On Your Positive Traits

Unscramble these terms, then use the bold letters to solve the puzzle to reveal a tip that can help you see the bright side of whatever situation you're in.

LEIXLFBE   _____

RGCANI   _____

OODG TNREELIS   _____

IEMCPATH   _____

AYLYTOL   _____

ELLBEIRA   _____

YSGGONIEA   _____

GOEFRIV SOHRET   _____

VEOL YASEIL   _____

MRMOCONITAUC   _____

_ _ _ _ _   _ _ _ _ _   _ _ _

Chase Your Dreams

Dreams often serve a purpose. For example, if you're dreaming of being in a certain place, with a specific person, or in a state of being that you've always imagined, your subconscious might be telling you to make that situation happen in real life! Turn those dreams into reality if it will boost your self-love and happiness. Write down some of your nighttime musings that could become daytime realities.

_____

_____

_____

_____

_____

_____

_____

_____

_____

_____

_____

_____

_____

_____

_____

Boost Your Brain Power

Even if you're not in school, you can still learn new things. Whether you take up a new hobby, read about an inspirational figure, or try to eat healthy foods, there are lots of ways to stimulate your brain.

ANALYZE
ASK
BOOK
CAFFEINE
CHOLINE
COFFEE

COGNITIVE
THINKING
CREATIVITY
CURIOSITY
EGGS
GROW

INSPIRE
INTELLIGENCE
LEARN
PROTEIN
QUESTION
READ

REFLECT
SLEEP MORE
WONDER

```
C G Q S X Q Q G Y U X P Z V C B T A
B O O R T K Y L N O I T S E U Q W Z
B Z G R O W J E J C N C X J R J L O
O A H N P G Z C R E A T I V I T Y M
H O X W I U A J A F N Z N B O O K H
Q M F I Z T J C F L O H T A S D E H
D D C E X F I E N T H M E A I R V J
X A R J X H I V R J C B L N T N K P
F E N R D N T R E O W Q L A Y Y T L
W H E K E I R V E T M I I L S G J V
Z A X F A E Z E X F H P G Y K G L A
D J A U F T N R A E L I E Z P D R W
P M Z Q W O N D E R S E N E X W C G
U Z T J C R C K E P C M C K L U J O
M U Q Q I P I N S P I R E T I S A E
Z N W V F I H A I A C H O L I N E H
W Z K H S V B K W B F V Y X S G G E
Z V V U U W Y O E D H L T A D C O Z
```

Build Confidence, Little by Little

If you want to increase your confidence, try to take small steps toward that goal. For example, go up to a stranger in a place where you can chat, such as a party, coffee shop, or neighborhood sidewalk. Strike up a conversation about a common interest or offer a compliment. Celebrate your courage in branching out, then write down your takeaways in your journal.

Find Beauty in Everyday Life

Beauty is around us all the time. Take a break from the business of life to appreciate beautiful things big and small, inside and out.

Across

1 Sea creature known for its beauty
3 Actress who wrote about "The Beauty of a Woman"
5 Home of the majestic lion
6 Makeup-free
8 Purple gemstone
11 Philosopher known for his "Theory on Beauty"
12 Heart of _____
13 Half; partly

Down

2 Opposite of outer
4 Christina Aguilera song
5 Sparkling gemstone
7 Painting, sculpture, etc.
9 Not brand-new
10 "Queen of the Garden"

Build Momentum

A mantra is a great tool for building self-love through repetition. Repeat this mantra when you wake up to set the tone for your day. The words will build confidence and momentum to get you out the door.

"I have the power to make today my greatest day yet. I deserve it."

Spread Your Wings

Come out of your cocoon! Spread your wings and color the butterflies as you imagine your beautiful, carefree self.

Splurge on Something Special

Unscramble these terms—all of which represent special ways to indulge yourself—then use the bold letters to solve the puzzle to find the category that all of these items fall under.

LTHOCAOCE FRFTU**SEL** _____

RWEOFL QTE**UU**OB _____

LJ**Y**EERW _____

YA**A**CTTOINS _____

NLANDEP P**R**IT _____

APS P**O**NTPAINETM _____

GI**B**EN WOSH _____

T**X**ARE PE**L**SE _____

THCAW _____

KLENE**A**CC _____

_ _ _   _ _ _ _   _ _ _ _   _ _ _ _

Thank Your Body

Your body does some truly amazing things every moment of the day. Take time to thank and appreciate every part by choosing an action from the first column and a body part from the second.

Knead	Feet
Thank	Shoulders
Relax	Legs
Hug	Core
Hold	Arms
Stretch	Hands
Touch	Back
Caress	Neck

Find Your Flow

In yoga practice, "flow" refers to how your mind can stay connected to your body and allow you to move throughout the poses and motions with a certain cadence and rhythm. "Finding your flow" in life works the same way. Keep your mind and body in sync to stay purposeful and balanced.

Grab your yoga mat and light a relaxing candle as you wind your way through this maze until you end up in a strong Warrior II Pose.

Forgive Yourself

After you find these words in the puzzle, look in a mirror and say "I forgive you" to yourself for something unresolved. Say it until you mean it! Everyone makes mistakes—show yourself the compassion you deserve.

ACCEPTANCE   FUTURE   LEARN LESSON   RECOGNIZE
BE BETTER   GOODBYE   LIBERATE   RELEASE
BLANK SLATE   HOPE   NEW   SELF-LOVE
COMPASSION   HUMAN   BEGINNING
FORGET IT   INNER   NEXT CHAPTER
FRESH START   KINDNESS   PAST

```
N O N J Y A U Z G C M L S Z B Z M S
Z U K S I E T H I F P E F K I M V C
L B E B E N F W U G U T E B Q A U L
Z P U Q F L N E E M S D D X N N T C
A E N B G W F E L S A G W I A O C V
J G T E W Y R L R R Q N I L Y J C O
Q J I B U K Q W O K L I E L D W K Y
P N T E P N X D E V I N Y E R J B L
P R E T P A H C T X E N B A A R Y M
C T G T I E H A L T A I D R C H J Y
U F R E S H S T A R T G O N C J K Z
Q R O R V S N L H O P E O L E N E Z
T U F J O E S X K F V B G E P S H V
Q E E M R K S S Q Q C W J S T A S B
D L Q U N R E L E A S E C S A D S K
P E T A R E B I L V Q N Y O N N P T
P U L L C O M P A S S I O N C M T N
F B O D W G M E Z I N G O C E R R R
```

Fight Fear

Think of a fear you have but want to face. Write a paragraph explaining where the fear comes from and what it's hindering, then brainstorm ways to confront and overcome it. Repeat this exercise as often as you like. When successful, record what worked and how it created positivity for you.

Seek Forgiveness

If you've done something you regret, you might want to apologize and ask for someone's forgiveness. Doing this can lighten the emotional burden you've been carrying and help you and the other party move on.

Across

1 Movie in which Anna Faris sings "Forgiveness"
4 Purple flower of forgiveness
5 "Be the _____ person"
8 Buddhist symbol of rebirth
9 Something you let go of
10 How koi swim: a direction

Down

2 Cut yourself some _____
3 "Heart of the Matter" singer
6 A _____ slate
7 Forgive and _____

Track Your Health

When you're constantly juggling work, various responsibilities, and personal relationships, your health can fall by the wayside. Unscramble these terms, then use the bold letters solve the puzzle to discover an idea that can help you keep track of how you're feeling every day.

ODOM   _____

IIOTUNNRT   _____

LMESUBR   _____

KOWTORU   _____

OVPIISTE HSUTGOHT   _____

LSMCHMOITCANPE   _____

OJB SLOAG   _____

HRPDEIIFSN   _____

SSESLON NAEDLRE   _____

_ _ _ _   _   _ _ _ _ _ _ _

Embrace the Wisdom of the Owls

There is great love, wisdom, and beauty inside you. Acknowledge your inner strengths and meditate on them as you color.

Sweat It Out

Self-love can come from a positive body image and comfort in your own skin. Try pairing an exercise-related activity from each column to work out and feel sweaty, strong, and accomplished.

Run...	in a group.
Walk...	outside.
Do an exercise video...	alone.
Jump...	with weights.
Lift...	while listening to music.
Swim...	inside.
Stretch...	in the morning.
Do high-intensity interval training...	with a resistance band.

Think Positively

Many of us spend too much time dwelling on negative thoughts and anxieties, whether they came from our own minds or the mouths of others. You can change negative thoughts into positive ones by changing your perspective and finding a silver lining. Step away from negative chatter and focus on your own perceptions.

On a day you're feeling down, start at the rainy corner of this maze, then follow the path through various ways to lift your mood until you reach the sunny ending.

Realize Your Fear Is Mental

Fear can become a mental block that hinders you from positive change—but you can fix it by becoming aware of it. Find the courage to embrace new experiences by pushing fear away and reshaping your mind. Repeat this affirmation to help train your brain to accept this new perspective. Do so until you feel ready and powerful.

"This fear is mental.
I am strong.
I am bold.
I will succeed."

Find a Path to Success

As you search for the words in this puzzle, think about three successes you've had and how they changed your life for the better.

ACCOMPLISHMENTS
AMBITION
BE PROUD
BRAINSTORM
BUILD
CHANGE
DRIVE

FIGHT FEAR
GAIN CONFIDENCE
JOURNEY
KEEP GOING
LEADERSHIP
MAKE PROFIT
MONEY

OBSTACLES
PLAN
POWER
REWARDS
TAKE RISKS
THRIVE

```
Q S E L C A T S B O X T L N J N T P
K T K I G B M Q J H H O I V O L K Z
G X B S C A M M D R E D E I U O S W
W G R K I O A O I R R T G R Z Y V
X O A D E R K V W D L I U B N L J B
P Z I I U E E Q C I B V H C E A R O
F K N L N O P K T M O E F R Y J H K
F T S H N C R G A A H W I E R Q D C
I N T M D X O P O T E B G W X M W S
G R O W H X F N E I L B D A N Q T X
H U R H H E I O F B N V O R P K K N
T F M C Z Q T B Q I G G C D C Q P A
F N M G P H T L E A D E R S H I P V
E U J D Q S B Z E F M E Y X J G L U
A C C O M P L I S H M E N T S F A W
R J B K S N U I E I N B L C Q K N M
T O V I O E R E W O P P S K E N R T
B L B L H J Q B M K M J V N T T O O
```

Self-Reflect

How you see yourself can affect how you feel. Take stock of yourself with this exercise. Draw two mirrors, side by side. In the first, draw an image of how you see yourself. In the second, draw how you envision your best self. What are the differences? If you're not feeling artistic, try just writing what you perceive as your flaws in the first mirror and the positive attributes you seek in the second.

Celebrate Your Power

Power can take on many forms—physical or spiritual. When difficult times arise, you'll need to call upon your power to push through and find peace. Unscramble these terms, then use the bold letters to solve the puzzle to reveal what you are every day, all day!

EECSIREINL   _____

CNOEUB CBKA   _____

VRVISOUR   _____

EPKE OGNIG   _____

GCEUORA   _____

GUTHO   _____

RCVOOEEM LCSABOSTE   _____

TNO KWAE   _____

RTEIHGF   _____

USCLEM OEWPR   _____

_ _ _ _   _ _ _ _ _ _

Find Your Inner Child

Youthful energy and a sense of playfulness can lead to new experiences that bring about self-discovery and a renewed burst of self-love. Give yourself those moments of childlike fun and adventure!

Take a break from working and solve this maze to remind yourself of elements of childhood that you should keep with you every day. When you finish, stand up and dance!

Let Go of Regrets

Everyone has regrets—it's okay to acknowledge them and let yourself feel whatever emotions come up alongside them.

- Write these regrets on a sheet of paper

- Then crumple it up and toss it in the trash

- Breathe

- Let the regret go

- Say to yourself, "I forgive myself"—and mean it

Love Your Body Through Nutrition

Create a week's worth of healthy meals and snacks using the words you'll search for in this puzzle.

ALMONDS
ANTIOXIDANTS
AVOCADO
BERRIES
BLACK BEANS
BROCCOLI
DARK CHOCOLATE

EDAMAME
EGG WHITES
FLAXSEED
FRESH FRUIT
IRON
LEAFY GREENS
OLIVE OIL

SALMON
SMOOTHIES
VEGGIES
WATERMELON
WHOLE GRAINS
YOGURT

```
E R H P Q H G E S E I H T O O M S P
C F H N X P L L A P D S P E C T K X
N M Y L I O E V I L O E W T N Y D Y
S O Z S P V A T U I P Y E A V S Z R
S N L J S Y F S W H N H D L Z N F G
M B I E D X Y F Q C G I A O Q C R X
M R H A M I G L J S X L M C F H C W
J F S V R R R V N O U O A O M R E T
F P D O S G E A I U V C M H C N T W
B Y N J B U E T U M A C E C Q I F B
L L O P W B N L A V D O Q K U V L E
J L M T K A S Q O W X R B R F R A R
W A L C O E G C J H X B F A Z L X R
T Y A V I W A S F F W H C D K E S I
K L P G I D N S H R S Z V S T P E E
B G G N O M L A S E G G W H I T E S
Q E I M T P B T R U G O Y N H C D R
V U E M Y X Q F G O S M Q K Z X V M
```

Use Visualization to Boost Confidence

Imagining a scene in your mind has been shown to help you make that idea a reality. Athletes often use this technique to imagine themselves performing well. Try this simple exercise in the morning before heading out the door to start your day on the right foot.

Close your eyes and take a deep breath. Inhale, then exhale. Visualize yourself walking down the street with style and confidence.

Accept Your Imperfections

No one is perfect. Stop holding yourself to that unrealistic standard and instead embrace all the parts of yourself. What you see as imperfections could actually be strengths if viewed in a different light. As you solve these clues, think of something you see as a flaw in yourself and turn it on its head by telling yourself that you love that trait.

Across
2 Permanent wounds
4 We are all _____
6 Weakness
8 Genuine
9 Buddhist symbol *enso*
11 Ending of a prayer
12 Singer of the lyric: "Just be perfectly imperfect"

Down
1 Opposite direction of west
2 Song by Taylor Swift
3 Good enough
5 One-of-a-kind
7 First name of the singer of "I Love Me"
10 A master at something

Overcome Common Challenges

Many obstacles can hold you back from finding self-love or happiness. Unscramble these terms to reveal obstacles, then use the bold letters to solve the puzzle to learn what you can find once you are able to move past them.

AAO**I**PNAR _____

TIS**P**TOEEIRNC**F** _____

TIRSSS**E** HECGNA _____

CNAOI**P**STTAINRRO _____

FSAT**E**DIME _____

NJTEEO**R**IC _____

AIEU**L**RF _____

NEMETTER**S**N _____

TINT**U**CNYERA _____

IOSNNEELLS _____

- - - -   - - - - - - -

Embrace Spontaneity

Some of life's greatest moments come from last-minute plans—or no plan at all! Instead of always needing a schedule or direction, let life and people take you to different places on a whim and see how it goes.

Step away from your to-do list and take a spontaneous trip somewhere fun. Enjoy the journey as much as the destination.

Learn from Your Mistakes

Mistakes are unavoidable—what's important is how you learn and grow from them. Write a short paragraph about a few recent mistakes, noting what you learned from them and how you'd act differently in the future. This practice will help you identify specific patterns so you can break the chain and implement different reactions to difficult situations.

Know That It's Okay If Some People Don't Like You

Rejection never feels good, especially since everyone craves acceptance to some degree. The key to self-acceptance is to love yourself for all your imperfections and quirks, and realize you don't need everyone to like you! Repeat this mantra when you are feeling upset that you might not be in sync with a particular person.

"If they don't like me, that's all right.
I am perfect just the way I am."

Change and Grow

As you color, remember that while change and growth
can be difficult, the rewards are worth it in the end.

Be Brave

As you solve these clues, remember a time when you were brave in the past, and think of a time when you may need to be brave in the near future.

Across

4   Encourage and assist
6   Take a chance
8   City in Nevada
10 Opposite of "go"
14 Desire to do something
15 Opposite of good
16 Do a good _____
20 力, the symbol of strength in this Japanese writing system
21 Rip
22 "Have I the courage to change?" singer
23 Song by Sara Bareilles

Down

1   Sturdy tree
2   Slightly open
3   To be forceful is to have an _____ will
5   Leave an area
7   Insult for someone lacking bravery
9   Bird known for courage
11 Team of animals pulling a plow
12 Brave female Disney character
13 Soothing, warm drink
17 Fire, water, air, and _____
18 Maya Angelou poem: "But still, like dust, I'll _____"
19 Remain

Increase Self-Love Through Reflection

Develop a deeper appreciation of and love for yourself by taking the time to reflect on your desires, qualities, dreams, and actions—both those from the past and those you wish to bring to life in the future. Pair an action from the first column with a theme from the second column to provide an outlet for reflection.

Change...	your mind.
Find...	your purpose.
Recite aloud...	your mantra.
Open or broaden...	your heart.
Create...	your direction.
Honor...	your meditation.
Re-evaluate...	your values.
Write about...	your home.

Radiate Inner Happiness

Let the words you are searching for in this puzzle help you focus on letting all the good things inside you radiate out.

AUTHENTICITY
BE NATURAL
BRIGHTEN
CHARM
GIGGLE
GLOW
GOOD MOOD

INFLUENCE
INSPIRE
JOKE AROUND
LAUGH
LIGHT UP
LIVE HAPPY
LOVE LIFE

POSITIVE ENERGY
RADIATE
SHINE
SMILE
SPARKLE

P T L H T N J J J Q J W C F L A C D
C O D U G O O D M O O D F W J H L X
Y D S A B Y J X X G K P Y O H Z T G
P T D I R Y M I E C N E U L F N I B
J L O S T E T E S Z N Y A G G G W W
P H I E F I L E V O L U A R G W O X
N I C C B K V L I Y T Z V L O F F I
Y R J H R Q J E Z H Z X E L X U I M
V J B A N C J B E N A T U R A L N Y
R T P R X E I N U N I L F U B U I D
J S T M I L T L I V E H A P P Y G H
B E Y B R I G H T E N R U B A G T H
U F N S C M T V N D A T G T O G Z T
O E R I P S N I X D H C Z Y L V I I
V M T U H Y V B I G P U D U J S D X
X Y W G Z S J A I M W H L F S N V N
D V W A Q Z T L E J V H W S B K K L
H I U H X E Z D T L M O T R U D G U

Make Good Things Happen

When you're getting ready to wow your colleagues in a meeting, dominate a workout, or take on some other tough task, recite this mantra to pump yourself up.

"I can do great things!"

Enjoy Gentle Touch

Unscramble these terms to learn various ways you can treat your body kindly, then use the bold letters to solve the puzzle and discover one way to manifest self-love.

SRAI**PE** _____

SNSIGIK _____

UU**HGH**FOTLT _____

LAESUNS _____

DL**O**H ADSHN _____

DN**Y**IKL _____

SGE**C**NRIAS _____

MAYRW**L** _____

AK**C**B BRU _____

RULAPSEE _____

MYT**A**NICI _____

_ _ _ _ _ _ _ _   _ _ _ _ _

Show Affection

There are so many different ways to show affection to yourself and others. Solve these clues to identify some unique options.

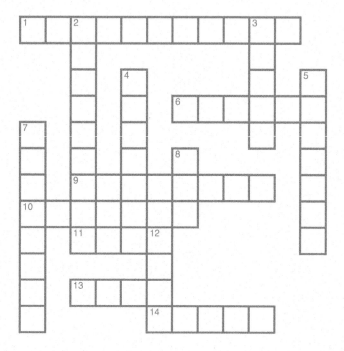

Across

1 A love language in Gary Chapman's book
6 Rose color for friendship
9 Three important words
10 Consume food
11 Level, not bumpy
13 Just right: chef's _____
14 One of the five senses

Down

2 Greek goddess of love
3 Type of leaf symbolizing unity and peace
4 Robert Burns: "My luve is like a red _____"
5 Type of massage
7 What two swans symbolize
8 Opposite of "no"
12 Place where birds live

Find Closure

It is impossible to move on after heartbreak if you have not received closure. To heal, forgive yourself for your errors and forgive those who may have wounded you as well. With forgiveness comes a clean slate, allowing you to put away the past and look toward the future. Breathe deeply as you contemplate these actions, and be gentle with yourself as you process and move forward.

Treat Yourself

An occasional treat can make life sweet,
and who deserves it more than you?

Embrace Life's Adventures

Stuck in a routine? Plan a solo trip—figure out the details, say what you hope to discover, and then develop action steps for your adventure.

ATTEMPT
CHANGE
CURIOUS
EAGERNESS
EXPERIENCE
FIND LOVE
FREEDOM

GLEE
HAVE FUN
INDEPENDENCE
MOVEMENT
OPENNESS
PLAY
POSITIVE MIND

RESILIENCE
SPONTANEOUS
STRENGTH
TAKE RISKS
VIVACIOUS
YOUTHFUL

```
W U A J J E M G K Y L Q P L A Y F T
L G F J Q F E M W S R T O S R A R Y
B T L V I V A C I O U S S W L Q C N
E Q F T X R M S N N N U I S M F D J
C Q I C R F K O G E O M T L M Q T S
U Q T K I S D I T E D R I D A V N H
G P N R N S U D N U E N V F N R B R
T P C Y P E T A E N A E E L G F S R
D W T T Q N T A G D W C M P E I N V
O F E R X N G T K K N N I C E N Y C
N Z Y G O E H A V E F U N F P D T U
N N G P R P V R I R R E D Z V L N R
P N S N D O J L E E I I L B Q O E I
B P E Y E J I E O R G U S B P V M O
E S M X B S D Z E T B N S K B E E U
S O K N E O T P M E T T A J S C V S
A X X R M D X M P Z L U F H T U O Y
N C F V I E B B B O T G X L C R M F
```

Get Rid of Toxicity

Toxic elements can decrease self-worth, making you feel stressed, small, and unworthy of kindness or respect. List the responsibilities, people, or events that no longer bring you happiness or help you be your best self. What is it about these people or things that causes you to behave in ways you don't like? With newfound self-awareness, find ways to detach or refocus your life in a healthier way.

Broaden Your Horizons

Your brain has no limit for knowledge, novel experiences, or self-discovery. Mix and match these actions and terms to come up with an activity that will boost your brain's function or provide some newfound wisdom or pleasure.

Try a new...	movie.
Recommend a...	skill.
Read an article about a...	theater performance.
Donate your time or effort to something related to a...	book.
Write down some thoughts about your favorite...	type of food.
Sketch something related to a...	piece of advice.
Teach yourself something related to a...	website.
Look for puzzles or games related to a...	museum.

Find Inner Peace

The path to inner peace is different for everyone. Solve these clues to find some ideas and items that can help evoke a sense of calm acceptance.

Across
1 Used to light lamps before electricity
5 Zodiac sign for balance
7 Branch indicating peace
9 Holder for the ball in golf
10 Yoga phrase
12 Katy Perry song about finding your own voice
14 Healing herb
15 Toy used to find fun in wintertime
18 Store event with big discounts
19 Peace of _____

Down
2 Opposite of movement
3 A lover, not a _____
4 Pronoun used by some who identify as women
6 Also known as
8 Gentle giant of the sea
11 Eating together is "breaking _____"
13 "_____ is just a number"
15 To be noticed is to feel _____
16 Bird of peace
17 Young boy

Be Mindful

Mindfulness is the act of living in the present moment and noticing what's around you through your senses. You can practice mindfulness through meditation, but you can also be mindful as you commute, exercise, or do a hobby or a chore. Unscramble these terms, then use the bold letters to solve the puzzle to find out what mindfulness can help you achieve.

ETDIA**E**TM   _____

GAYO RTAE**P**CIC   _____

LGNMA**I**C   _____

LN**Y**IRUTQIAYT   _____

ERCAL NIDM   _____

RLTCEFINO**E**   _____

OTJ **N**OWD   _____

BA**H**TEER   _____

COSUF   _____

RONTATCCOINNE   _____

– – – – – – – – – –

Declutter Your Home

Having a clean space can lead to your mind feeling less cluttered as well. Choose one area of your home that's been bothering you, and see if you can donate, recycle, or trash anything in it. Then treat yourself to a new item to spruce up that space so you enjoy spending time there.

Let Your Light Shine

Never forget how radiant you are.
Appreciate and honor your talents as you color these stars.

Write a Paragraph from a Book about Yourself

Pretend you are writing a book about yourself that promotes self-love! Give it a title, then write a short introductory paragraph explaining the premise, the character, and what the reader can take away from this heartwarming, influential book.

_____

_____

_____

_____

_____

_____

_____

_____

_____

_____

_____

_____

_____

_____

_____

Feel Comfortable Being Alone

Spending time alone can be rewarding, as it frees you from external distractions and stress and lets you focus on what you like to do best. Do whatever makes you happy and comfortable with your own company. Brainstorm activities, such as eating a meal alone, going for a short walk in nature, or taking in a movie on your own.

Get Ready to Glow

Your inner beauty shines through when you feel like your best self. Radiate positive energy and shine as you take each step throughout the day. Recite this affirmation each morning to put yourself in an upbeat frame of mind.

"My inner glow is strong.
I will brighten lives today."

Keep Stress Low

As you search for the words in this puzzle, work on incorporating these ideas into your daily routine—perhaps make a morning and evening ritual using two options.

BATH
BE CALM
BREATHE
DANCE
EXERCISE
GO OUTSIDE
JOURNALING

ME TIME
MEDITATE
MOVIE
NAP
PEACEFUL
READ BOOK
RUN

SAY NO
SEND TEXT
SMILE
STRETCH
VACATION
WALK

```
C N V E H J F C P R O I Z B Z W K P
G W V F O O A I I I Q N M U Y D D T
E M K T M U Q Z Q H I J Z D Y N J O
X U R X A E S C T W D U B R J G C W
E K M E D I T A T E I M B K X R B Q
R Y U T C O B I Y A T T Z P B P M B
C M U D R N U P M N N D A I R V P H
I O G N P P A B D E O R T M H M W R
S J N E N N P D S E Y F N C F O M S
E D I S T U O O G E H O T I P F C C
L M L A C E B C T Z I E K U X Z P F
R E A D B O O K U T R V L C Y G U A
W D N G K B R E A T H E O I K H H R
C U R F S L Z C S C B F V M M Z R X
R L U F E C A E P A N G S Q G S X R
C X O H Z V N W X A L C Z J W G G U
F C J H V M Q S T S G A Y K B F W A
X L N O L G A V A Z I P D A X B R O
```

Treat Yourself Like You'd Treat a Friend

One way to prioritize self-love is to treat yourself like you'd treat a friend. Be kind to yourself when you're hurting, think of little things to do for yourself when you're in a funk, and be gentle with yourself when you make a mistake.

Splurge on Yourself

Every once in a while, find little ways to indulge in simple pleasures or even splurge on gifts or experiences you've had your eyes or heart set on. For example, book a massage, enjoy dark chocolate, schedule a workout or date, buy a gift you deserve and can afford, or have a glass of wine. Write some notes about how the experience made you feel.

Know Your Truth

Hearing someone say something untrue about you can impair your perception of yourself. Counteract that gossip by identifying, respecting, and living by your truth. Repeat this mantra to drown out the noise.

"I know my truth, and I feel good about it—that's all that matters."

Be a Positive Influence

Showing love to people you care about is another way to be your authentic self. Could anyone in your life benefit from your guidance, friendship, or support right now? As you solve the clues for this puzzle, think about how you can be a positive influence on someone else.

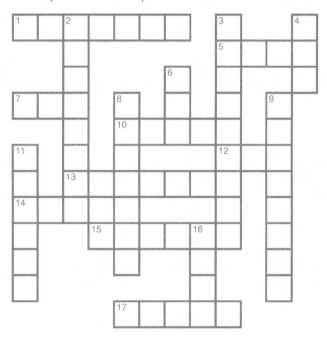

Across
1   American Civil Rights activist Jesse _____
5   Muslim caliph from the sixth century
7   Small hotel
10 "Listen and_____"
12 A large unit of weight
13 Song by John Lennon
14 A type of bread
15 Trusted guide
17 Symbol of protection, strength, and courage

Down
2   Early American philanthropist
3   Donate your time
4   Limb connected to the shoulder
6   The biological sequence that makes you who you are
8   "Today a reader, tomorrow _____ _____"
9   Think of new things
11 Color for royalty
16 Smell

Get Savvy in the Kitchen

If you feel daunted by the prospect of cooking healthy meals, try other simple techniques like meal prep, freezing dishes to thaw and eat later, and ordering out every once in a while. Mix and match the cooking ideas in the left column with the foods in the right column to offer yourself a variety of new, nutritious dishes to enjoy all week long.

Try a new recipe that uses...	protein.
Cook...	chocolate.
Cook your favorite recipe that includes...	wine.
Meal prep a dish that calls for...	rice.
Order a dish from a local restaurant that features...	veggies.
Discover a new way to prepare...	eggs.
Buy prepared food from a grocery store that uses...	soup.
Freeze a meal that includes...	fruit.

Reflect and Improve

Use these boxes for a quick self-reflection writing exercise. In the first box, write down some skills you excel in. In the second, write down a few skills you'd like to improve upon. In the third, brainstorm a few ideas for how you can bolster the skills you'd like to improve.

Find Romance

Part of loving yourself can include being in a romantic relationship that helps you be your best self. Unscramble these romantic terms to put you in the mood for a special date with your partner, or to send good vibes out into the universe to find just the right person for you. Then use the bold letters to solve the puzzle and discover something you can say to your partner when the time is right—or to yourself, anytime!

ALHEFTERT   _____

TEAD HINGT   _____

CMNTOIAR   _____

VYLGINLO   _____

WEENR SOWV   _____

MAOSIDDN   _____

GOIOWN   _____

RMECEAB   _____

NETAGGEEMN   _____

LMUSTOAE   _____

— — — — — — — — — — — — —

Stay True to Yourself

Use your internal desire for improvement to spur you to change—not the influence of outsiders who don't understand your truth. Repeat this mantra when in doubt, or under pressure from others to stray from who you truly are.

"I change for myself."

Trust Your Instincts

Even when you feel unsure about a decision or situation, you can probably sense what you should do. Try to quiet your mind and get in touch with your inner self as you solve the clues for this puzzle.

Across
2 Not old
5 Intuition
6 Unit for measuring land
9 Have an inkling
10 Celestial body in the sky
12 It just feels _____

13 Albert Einstein: "The only real _____ thing is intuition"

Down
1 Leaping insect
3 Dean Koontz: "Intuition is seeing _____ _____"

4 Singer of the lyric "I'm gonna follow my intuition"
7 Wonder about
8 Trust your _____ voice
11 Green pod used in gumbo

Let the Little Things Slide

When you're feeling overwhelmed or anxious, little things can seem huge. But don't let missing one workout or forgetting to buy milk at the store send you spiraling. Take a deep breath, realize that life will go on, and remind yourself of all the amazing things you do on a daily basis.

Feel the Sunlight

You know that warm, tingly feeling you get when you're sitting outside on a lounge chair in the sun? Even if it's not sunny right now, you can still give yourself a similar vibe by visualizing the experience. Close your eyes and visualize the sun gently warming every part of your body.

Limit Things That Suck Your Energy

Even as you look to do more of what you love, you can look to see if you should do less of anything. Use this list as a starting point to ask yourself if you have habits or foods that you could minimize. Pick five things and make action steps to reduce their prevalence in your life.

ALCOHOL
ANXIETY
BAD ENERGY
CANDY
FAST FOOD
FRYING
INSECURITIES

LONELINESS
NEGATIVE TALK
OVERANALYZING
PROCESSED JUNK
REGRET
RUMINATION
SELF-DOUBT

SODA
STRESS
SUGAR
SWEETENER
TOXIC PEOPLE
WHITE BREAD

```
A U F R C R A B P S W E E T E N E R
J O F Z G N I Y R F P Y P I E C A A
N B P S E L F D O U B T E G L C J G
W O R M H W H A C T A A A N P S F U
G W I E C M G A E Z S T N I O R N S
F Q F T G N P P S D I D X Z E O O E
B J N S A R M F S V N C I Y P S H L
P P O Y T N E K E I S P E L C S S Y
I L F T A M I T D S E M T A I E T W
L X P A H H A M J Y C Q Y N X N H O
Q P O L S L E C U G U M Q A O I Z G
E B O C K T A F N R R O V R T L H Y
U R E O P X F C K E I T R E Z E D W
N A N H S N U O G N T V B V X N D C
R R E O Q N L V O E I R R O A O B K
B J D L O O Q C O D E Z M C N L E W
E A G U G J M N K A S T R E S S S T
M S N E N G P M D B C G R J A X O O
```

Find Self-Love Through Improvements in Self-Care

Finding different ways to love yourself will give you more tools for keeping yourself happy and healthy. Take an activity from the first column and pair it with a frequency or method from the second column to give yourself new ideas for experiencing more happiness and relaxation on a daily basis.

Sleep...	longer.
Laugh...	faster.
Smile...	easier.
Love...	harder.
Breathe...	deeper.
Feel...	alone.
Indulge...	better.
Appreciate...	with a friend or partner.

Spread Your Wings

Imagine you're one of these birds and use your wings to fly wherever your heart desires. As you color, visualize yourself reaching your goals.

Embrace Your Intuition

When you trust your gut, you're more likely to make decisions that are in line with your values and truths. Try these two ideas to strengthen your relationship with your intuition when you're faced with a difficult decision or situation:

- Close your eyes and visualize yourself in the scenario. What choice does the pretend you make in the moment?

- Write down all possible decisions on different pieces of paper. Start to toss them in the trash, starting with what you feel least comfortable with. Which is the last to remain?

Celebrate Your Work Accomplishments

A thriving career provides purpose, and it's probably how you spend much of your week. Let your work lift you up and create pride and ambition! Write down an accomplishment or two that you experienced at work. Be sure to celebrate it—maybe get drinks with friends or bake yourself a cake—no matter how small the accomplishment.

Own Your Worth

Owning your worth also relates to feeling confident and proud. Think about your worth as you solve this puzzle.

Across
2 Price _____ pound
4 Request something
7 Floating on _____
8 Molten rock
10 "King of the jungle"
12 Ariana Grande song "_____ Rings"
15 Fictional company in old cartoons
16 To be alone is to fly_____
18 Soothing plant
19 Male child
20 Barbra Streisand quote: "Confidence and _____ are at two ends of the scale, and you need both"

Down
1 How to stand
3 Opposite of common
5 Song by Hailee Steinfeld
6 Hold dear
7 Small unit of matter
9 Opposite of insecure
11 Currency in Mexico
13 Short sleep
14 Lizzo song "Good As _____"
17 Don't settle for_____

Swap Shame for Laughter

When you're embarrassed, it's easy to recoil or want to hide. Instead, brush it off and laugh about it—let those who witnessed it join in too. Keep the vibes positive and show that you love yourself even in those not-so-perfect moments.

Find Your Purpose

Finding your purpose doesn't have to feel intimidating. Start by thinking about what makes you excited or motivated. Unscramble these terms, then use the bold letters to solve the puzzle and reveal what you're looking for in a purpose.

DNIPSREI   _____

KCAWSEUTR   _____

LFSLUUT   _____

GICAMTEN   _____

GRBAEHTTKANI   _____

FFCOUREL   _____

RLAPPUO   _____

TUSM EAHV   _____

REDBLESIA   _____

GNEUIRTI   _____

_ _ _ _ _ _ _ _   _ _ _ _ _ _

Produce a Rom-Com

Who doesn't love a rom-com that gives you the feels and touches your heart? Create a rom-com for your personal life, where you are the star. Imagine the trailer—give it a beginning and purpose, a journey with ups and downs that shaped you, and a happy ending, of course. Write down your ideas.

Trust Your Intuition

Your intuition is most valuable in decision-making. That gut instinct senses what's right and best for you, so let it lead you without second-guessing. Repeat this mantra when you're torn.

"I feel what's right in my gut and my heart. Take a leap. Trust."

Find Ways to Recharge

It's inevitable—sometimes we drain our energy stores and need to recharge. Whether through a warm bath, binge-watching a show, or taking a nap or a walk outside, find ways to uplift your mood and feel rejuvenated.

When your battery is low, find your way through this maze, letting the key words recharge you until your battery is full again.

Get Creative

Mixing and matching these terms will give you ideas for activities that can spark your creativity—through writing or photography, for example—in order to build confidence and find more positivity in your life.

Illustrate	Photo
Post	Compliment
Collage	Energy
Revise or improve	Positivity
Share	Mantra
Recite	Poem
Write	Balance
Reflect	Relaxation

Dream Big

Write down a dream you have and its meaning to you. After you find the words in this puzzle, create five action steps to make your goal a reality.

ADVENTURE
ASPIRE
BOLDNESS
CONFIDENCE
CREATIVITY
DETERMINATION
FEARLESS

HOPEFUL
IMAGINE
INNOVATE
INSPIRE
PASSION
PATIENCE
PERSEVERANCE

PERSISTENCE
PIVOT
SET GOALS
SUCCESS
THINK BIG
TRY HARDER

```
A J Q P O B N I E X K D X F M X E T
A V Y B E O G M Q P Y E L K P X R Q
P O U B Z S L A O G T E S E C B I Q
F X A M K J X T O V I P R I N L P L
B I L Y N X H L A P V S U C C E S S
L O C F M E C N E D I F N O C A A S
W S L Q E W I N C S T E G V C H A S
T U Q D C J I N T C A C I S M D P N
L I F R N G Z E R T E N B S V B K B
F V N V A E N B Y Z R E K E J D Q A
E Q O M R C S N H L C I N L U E S D
W T I L E E C S A B B T I R G T L K
F X S P V P X C R P U A H A X A H E
S F S U E W Y L D R R P T E A V K J
F Y A G S L U F E P O H Q F V O F Q
J K P F R I U E R I P S N I W N W D
A R W D E T E R M I N A T I O N O M
R C R U P P G T M I N Y Z I J I Z X
```

Increase Open-Mindedness

List five things you have wanted to do but are hesitant to try. Explain why you are fearful or uncertain, and then express why you wish to have this new experience. Finally, make a plan to give it a shot!

1: _____

2: _____

3: _____

4: _____

5: _____

Eat Better to Improve Your Well-Being

The foods you choose to eat have a huge impact on your mind and body. Healthy picks improve mood and quality of life, which can then boost self-love and confidence. Consider refining your meals by focusing on high-quality proteins like lean beef, chicken breast, fish, Greek yogurt, cottage cheese, beans/legumes, soy, whole grains, leafy greens, root vegetables, nuts, and seeds.

Follow Your Wildest Dreams

Don't get bogged down by logistics as you imagine big things for yourself. Every obstacle can be overcome with the right combination of dedication and opportunity. As you solve these clues, imagine your wildest dream.

Across
5   Tupac Shakur quote: "Dreams are _____"
7   Fabergé _____
8   Strong male Disney character
11 Animal that represents love, loyalty, and protection
12 Think outside the _____
14 Molecule with a net electric charge
15 Celestial symbol of inspiration

Down
1   _____ for the course
2   Be creative and use your _____
3   Animal symbol of playfulness and imagination
4   *Moana* singer of "How Far I'll Go"
6   Eminem lyric: "You only get one _____"
9   Color of passion and courage
10 "Don't Stop Believin'" band
13 Leave out

Collect Love from Others

If you're struggling to find self-love, look to others for help. Ask trusted friends or family members to list your positive qualities, as sometimes we fail to see these in ourselves or are unaware of the wonderful impact we can have on those we care for. Then feel that self-love!

Make Lemonade

Acknowledge your troubles and setbacks. As you color this page, reflect on a time you made lemonade when life gave you lemons.

Heal Through Self-Care

Whether you need to heal your body, mind, or spirit, focusing on yourself is a great place to start. Schedule some of these activities into your week with set calendar appointments.

COMPASSION
DATING
FORGIVE YOURSELF
HUMAN TOUCH
JOURNALING
LAUGHTER
MASSAGE

MEDITATION
MUSIC
OPENNESS
PROCESS
RESILIENCE
SEE FAMILY
SLEEP

SMILE
SOCIALIZE
SPA DAY
SWEAT
WARM BATH
YOGA

```
D M L M P S Y F T S Q M F V X N X A
Z C E G Z E I M E V C E L I M S W S
S I Q K S Q B E D O Y D B S L X R I
P S V K I B F F M F C I A Q E E W U
A U E F H A N P O Q S T K V S C A F
D M Z C M C A S O C I A L I Z E S B
A Z O I O S U F U A J T L H S J Y U
Y F L E S R U O Y E V I G R O F L Y
A Y B I S L P Z T E E O F U U N T A
A G O G L W A S C N R N R U K R Y B
H N A T E N R F C W A N N X E O N H
S I O P E N N E S S A M U T G Z M D
J T F W P F D G T L X R U A A N X S
F A W X G L Q D I H N W M H S F W C
G D V F O N T N V Y G L T B S E Q R
G M G M H U G X A D A U W F A Y W D
Z U F C I M S C W C X C A T M T D O
U J T Q X X U T M E C W V L F J H H
```

Know Your Worth

Obstacles come our way, disagreements and conflicts arise—in these times, you may feel unmoored or confused, especially about your self-worth. Yet even when you feel unsure, you are worthy of love and happiness. To remind yourself of this, look in the mirror at your reflection. Smile. Let your mouth return to neutral and hold your gaze. Repeat the following affirmation every morning while you fight through the pain and heal.

"I am strong.
I am confident.
I am above this."

Seize Your Opportunities

Sometimes your next big move comes from saying yes when opportunity knocks. As you solve these clues, remind yourself that you are brave and ready for your next challenge.

Across

1 Quote author: "Self-care is not selfish"
3 Harmonious
6 Movie with Jim Carrey
7 The Beehive State
9 "Just Say Yes" band
10 Prophetic event
14 Make more important

Down

2 Slippery fish
4 C.J. Langenhoven quote: "Yes is like _____"
5 Latin for "Seize the day"
8 Try something new
10 Keep an _____ mind
11 Type of snake
12 None
13 A sibling, for short

Connect with Others for Loving Relationships

Maintaining healthy relationships with others is one way to love yourself. If you have a strong and supportive social network, you will likely have greater self-love as well. Pair an action from the left column with an idea from the right column to brainstorm some ideas for developing and fostering relationships.

Plan your own...	party.
Accept someone's invitation to a...	charity event.
Invite a new friend to a...	Zoom meeting.
Grab an old friend for a...	museum trip.
Join a family member for a...	hike.
Ask a colleague (if appropriate) to go to a...	meal.
Strike up a conversation with someone at a...	class.
Share something new about yourself at a...	coffee date.

Show Off Your New Talents

Open your mind to new activities that you might excel in. Knitting? Woodworking? Dancing? Cooking? Think of where you can hone your skills and develop a talent you can be proud of!

You're a star! Dive into this maze and remind yourself of all the talents you already have and think of a new skill to try.

Know That It's Okay (and Good!) to Change Yourself with Time

While you should be authentic and love yourself as you are right now, it's also good to work on continually being curious, embracing change and adventure, and discovering new interests. Think about something you've already changed about yourself, and jot down some thoughts about how the change made you feel. Now note a change you're looking forward to making in the future.

Have Fun with Your Outer Beauty

Of course, your inner beauty is what's most important and where you should focus a lot of your energy. But it's also okay to play with your outer beauty as well! Plan a fun occasion where you can get glammed up! Think of what you'll wear as you find these words.

APPEARANCE
BEAUTIFUL
BIG SMILE
BLOWOUT
BLUSH
CHIC
DRESS UP

FANCY
FASHION
FEEL SEXY
GLAMOUR
GLITTER
GLOSS
HIGH HEELS

LASHES
LIPSTICK
STYLE
TRENDY
UPDO
WHITE TEETH

```
Y Y Y I R K A R V K J R P K N H Y I
P D R E S S U P W S T Q R Y J F X V
R N U G O W T G P M V L I T K E E X
U E W H I T E T E E T H P G L O S S
O R O L B P Z W B E A U T I F U L A
H T L D A V G G A L G R M M C V E Y
F C H O P Y C A K C O S A H I S E S
U Z G B R U O M A L G W L N H L F U
B A A N X R E T T I L G O A C E D C
G K O Z O F L Y B R B I C U S E Q D
Y Z O E K X Y T C O J I P L T H Q S
L V Y G J K T X R N U J T S Y H E W
U O W M B D S N Z G A Y H S T G K S
D T S Y O K K P M P O F A S H I O N
S Y C D T Y O K J N X A R P U H C T
O P M P L G G T N N N T G S R L O K
V U O F A E L N E C V T M N C V B T
Y B J X O G C E S O F R N W M X B L
```

Feel Happier

Happiness looks like different things to different people. As you solve these clues, ask yourself what or who makes you happy, and make a point to regularly incorporate those things or people into your life.

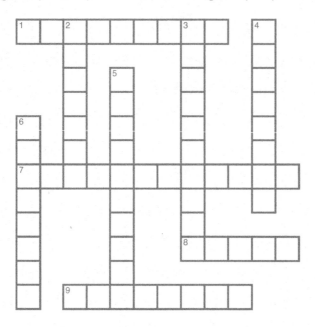

Across
1 Blossom of warmth
7 Eight-spoked wheel of Buddhism
8 Opposite of frown
9 Hormone for love

Down
2 Buddhist destination
3 Mood-boosting hormones
4 Winged symbol of happiness
5 Charles M. Schultz book: "Happiness Is _____ _____"
6 "Laughter is the best _____"

Boost Your Mood

Try as we may to stay positive all the time, that's not realistic. Sometimes, we all feel a little blue and need a pick-me-up. Unscramble these terms for some ideas that can help you brighten your outlook, then use the bold letters to solve the puzzle to discover an important chemical that you want to keep in check.

PIN**O**DAM**E** _____

OORNNIT**S**E _____

YLCGC**I**N _____

TIATDUERG EELT**R**T _____

XCIN**O**YTO _____

EFCA ME**I**T _____

BB**L**EUB TAHB _____

APYP**H O**RHU _____

AEP**MI**N**T** _____

GELUTAH**R** _____

– – – – – – – – –   – – – – – – –

Write a Gratitude Letter to a Loved One

You can build self-love by showing love to others, especially those whom you appreciate in your inner circle. It brightens their day and warms their heart—and then does so for you too. You can email or text them this letter, but a handwritten version with a photo of you two accompanying it would be extra special.

Nourish Your Body to Nourish Your Soul

Eating different colored fruits and vegetables helps keep your mind and body sharp. As you color, meditate on your favorite healthy foods.

Act Like a Leader

Taking charge of a situation you're knowledgeable about can help boost your confidence. Think about a time when you led effectively in the past—or could lead effectively in the future—as you find these words.

ACHIEVE
ACT
ADAPT
BUILD
CHANGE
COMMAND
CONNECTIONS

COURAGE
DOMINATE
DREAM
EXPAND
GROW
INFLUENCE
INITIATE

POSITIVE THINKING
POWERFUL
SAY YES
SPARK
STRENGTH
TAKE CHARGE

```
L U E I O H C N S J T S F F W M Y Y
L O K Y G D B S A H I R V O R W B F
Y S X K X M K I Y J T M R B D I O E
V O T M H U Z D Y E F G F B G W B W
N P O S I T I V E T H I N K I N G F
H O F I N E A J S C O O K E I L T T
D K W Y G O H K D C W K V O R D L T
X M R U I P I T E L K E P A C T O D
M Z B A W G V T Z C I E Z C U A S A
T D N A P X E T C H H U W V M I C H
F C Q U J S T P C E S A B Q E M D L
H H O I W J A A A N N A R G N O W P
W A D M W B I D J A D N A G M K D Y
Q N D Q M B T A U K V R O I E R X M
W G W W V A I N F L U E N C E M X C
R E J U D B N G F O T A B A J K F O
O M Z Q D O I D C Y T Z M L R G V Q
Z G I M D S P O W E R F U L G B Z U
```

Eliminate Toxic Elements

Negative influences can affect your life no matter how hard you try to avoid them. When you notice them creeping in, take a deep breath and tell yourself not to engage. Unscramble these terms to reveal toxic elements you might encounter, then use the bold letters to solve the puzzle to see what to do with those elements.

SPGIO**S** _____

AREF _____

AVIETN**G**E LKTA _____

UT**D**B**O** _____

RSUG**G**DE _____

LEYASJU**O** _____

TAHNU**Y**ELH TSP**R**O**L**EAINHSI _____

A**BD** EBVIS _____

RNUT**Y**SIICE _____

AIMIN**O**NS _____

– – –   – – – – –   – – –   – – –

Write a Letter to Your Younger Self

Write a letter to your younger self, expressing what you wish you had known back then or which dreams you had that would come true. Now imagine what your future self would tell your current self, focusing on your limitless potential.

Unwind after a Long Day

When you've been running from one thing to the next all day, it's important to find time to transition into nighttime so you can get quality rest. If you don't take time to wind down, you might find your mind racing all night as you try to process your day. Choose an activity from the left column and an idea from the right column to build a bedtime routine that is calming, centering, and restful.

Snuggle with a blanket...	near safely lit candles.
Relax...	while listening to a quiet playlist.
Dance...	while enjoying aromatherapy.
Bathe...	after practicing deep breaths for several minutes.
Play a solitary card game...	before meditating for five minutes.
Stretch...	in a warm room.
Drink a cup of herbal tea...	then apply lotion to your arms and legs.
Write in your journal...	while looking forward to restful sleep.

Celebrate Friendship

Friends are there for you through thick and thin, good times and bad. As you solve these clues, think about good friends you have now, and consider the ways that you are a good friend to others.

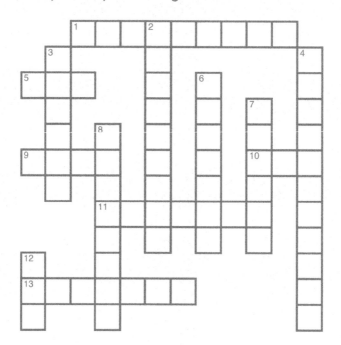

Across
1 Jewelry passed between friends
5 Professional boxer and activist Muhammad _____
9 Majestic forest animal
10 Clever; crafty
11 Proverbs 27:9: "Sweet friendships refresh _____ _____"
13 Well-liked

Down
2 Opposite of lonely
3 Chrysanthemum or daisy
4 "You Got a Friend in Me" singer
6 Maya Angelou: "Be a _____ in someone else's cloud"
7 Me, _____, and I
8 Thankful
12 Choose

Learn to Love Change

Change can be hard—the fear of the unknown can be paralyzing at times. After all, it's safe and easy to stick with what's familiar. Yet change can be a blessing in the long run after you overcome the discomfort. Think of a life situation you wish to change and why. How might it lead to self-love?

Let It Go

Imagine your worries are hot-air balloons ready to take off. Send them up into the atmosphere as you color, and feel liberated and calm.

See Self-Love Through the Eyes of Others

To love others, you must love yourself first. If you are struggling to find self-love, consider the reasons other people in your life love you—and they do, a lot! Remind yourself of those reasons while you recite this mantra.

"People love me for a reason.
I am good.
I am kind. I am me."

Write a Letter to Your Future Self

Take a few moments today and write a letter to your future self that celebrates where you are now in life. Include details of your current job, what you see as your purpose and passions, upcoming goals you want to achieve, and what you're most proud of at the moment.

Hang Out with a Friend

These paired activities are super fun to do with a buddy, so you both can feel healthier and happier together as a means to promote greater self-love. And you'll likely develop a deeper connection with each other too!

Play a board game...	somewhere outside.
Cook or eat a meal...	somewhere inside.
Take a bike ride...	at a local park.
Volunteer...	somewhere in between both your homes.
Go for a walk...	in the grass.
Have a cup of coffee...	near some hills or mountains.
Dance...	by some water.
Laugh at a funny memory...	in a garden.

Indulge in Life's Simple Pleasures

There are lots of ways to show yourself love on a daily basis. As you find the words in the puzzle, seek to implement at least one of these treats into your day.

CANDLES
CARDIO
CHOCOLATE
COMPLIMENTS
DATE NIGHT
DESSERT
FRIENDSHIP

GIFTS
HOLIDAY
LAZY SUNDAY
NOURISHMENT
PERFUME
SAUNA
SELF-CARE

SEX
STREAMING
SUNSHINE
VACATION
WEEKEND
WINE

```
P T D M U I O J T S E L U L V P Q J
S T L O J Y P M L H P W G I T N L B
X M C Z S E F X V A G V C V E I S A
L T D E R M X R H I Z I M B W U Q O
J H G F P M K R I U P Y N Q G O T R
G P U D J T Z A G E T G S E S G D N
I M W S A U N A O K N U D U T R M L
E C G I V D W E C I R D E P N A L Q
S N X A N G W R M C D S S B E D D A
H X I I W E X A J H S R Y H M G A N
T O V H E E E C F O S V A A I X J Y
X R L K S R A F O C V I R C L P G L
G B E I T N Z L K O T Q R R P Y O X
P N R S D M U E K L N G X U M V P F
D U F L S A J S V A C A T I O N A Z
Y M E X P E Y F S T F I G C C N O U
Y S I L N H D E I E I O L N O W G Y
D V A R M B Z S P U D L A O L U A A
```

Be Yourself

There's no one in the world like you—celebrate that! Unscramble these terms as you focus on the wonder of you, then use the bold letters to solve the puzzle for a phrase you can think about as you celebrate your uniqueness.

PSN**E**SN**EO**   _____

EAVH ST**U**TR   _____

ESAREEL ONTNSII**HB**II   _____

CE**N**PESEREXI   _____

EUN**T**DARVE   _____

KET**A S**KRSI   _____

ME**A**TTTP   _____

UIYRTO**C**SI   _____

NOJEU**Y**R   _____

NIGBE E**T**RSEPN   _____

– – – – – – – – – –   – –   – – –

Make a Wish

As you color the cakes and candles, remember that every day is a new day to dream and celebrate life's magic.

Strengthen Your Body

Exercise boosts endorphins, which can improve mood and keep chronic stress low. Regularly sweating through cardio and strength training may also improve your body image, so you feel beautiful and strong. Be sure to take time to put your body first and engage in whatever exercise makes you happy.

Give and Receive

Anyone who volunteers their time for others knows that giving back benefits both the giver and the receiver. Contemplate how service can improve your life and the lives of others as you solve these clues.

Across
4 Give in return
5 Kind word
6 Trade
7 "Give a Little Bit" band
8 Gift

Down
1 Acts of service, for example
2 Holiday figure bearing gifts
3 Singer of "Wind Beneath My Wings"
6 Opposite of one-sided

Feel Comfortable in Your Own Skin

Your body is beautiful, and it is unique. Feeling confident, free, and proud can help you build more self-love in your life. Embrace and celebrate your body by dancing in front of the mirror, sitting in a sauna, taking a bath, photographing yourself, or moisturizing your skin.

Work Together

Loving yourself sometimes means taking care of yourself as you work in a group. Unscramble these terms to learn key components to good cooperation, then use the bold letters to solve the puzzle to discover a description of a healthy group.

CPRPAAOAHLBE   _____

NYSTOHE   _____

LUTMAU ETSPREC   _____

TURTS   _____

UANLRTA SBEIV   _____

LOMOCMYTIAN   _____

FEFTRO   _____

LAYTIQU MIET   _____

MIEMSORE   _____

MKAETORW   _____

_ _ _ _ _ _ _   _ _ _ _ _ _

Psych Yourself Up

A mantra is a great tool for building self-love through repetition. Repeat this mantra each day upon waking up to set the tone for the day ahead. It will build confidence and self-worth.

"I can accomplish anything
I set my mind to.
Dream big.
I got this."

Break a Sweat

Movement is one of the best antidotes to stress. Think of your favorite ways to get a little exercise to boost your mood as you color in this picture.

Embrace the Power of No

While saying yes to new opportunities for growth, adventure, and fun can make for the greatest experiences, it's also important to learn the power of no, so you avoid overtaxing yourself with too many obligations. Set aside some downtime for yourself too! In the next week, try saying no to a request that you can't fulfill.

Look Ahead

While you should celebrate who you are right now, it's also wise to look ahead sometimes. What do you envision your future looking like? Reach for the stars as you unscramble these motivating terms, then use the bold letters to solve the puzzle.

PNIA**C**TITANO**I** _____

XLEAIP**N**EONT _____

T**T**PIOIMS _____

FLA**H** FLLU _____

GE**E**SEARNS _____

EEF**R** STII**R**P _____

GESESL**A** _____

YASSPNLFUL**E** _____

SSPUOOT**N**ANE _____

VY**T**NOEL _____

_ _ _ _   _ _ _ _ _ _ _

ANSWERS

Cultivate Beauty from Within (p. 10)

Empower Yourself (p. 15)

Boost Your Confidence (p. 12)

- **Words:** praise, positive talk, mantra, affirmations, self-worth, bold, good attitude, love yourself, extroverted, sociable
- **Answer:** A powerful vibe

Follow Your Heart (p. 13)

Create More Wealth (p. 17)

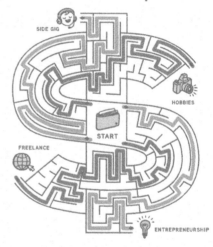

Explore Feelings of Touch (p. 20)

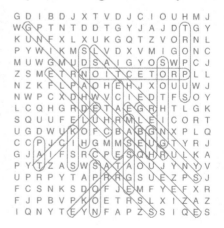

Focus On Your Positive Traits (p. 24)

- **Words:** flexible, caring, good listener, empathic, loyalty, reliable, easygoing, forgive others, love easily, communicator
- **Answer:** Smile every day

Boost Your Brain Power (p. 26)

Find Beauty in Everyday Life (p. 28)

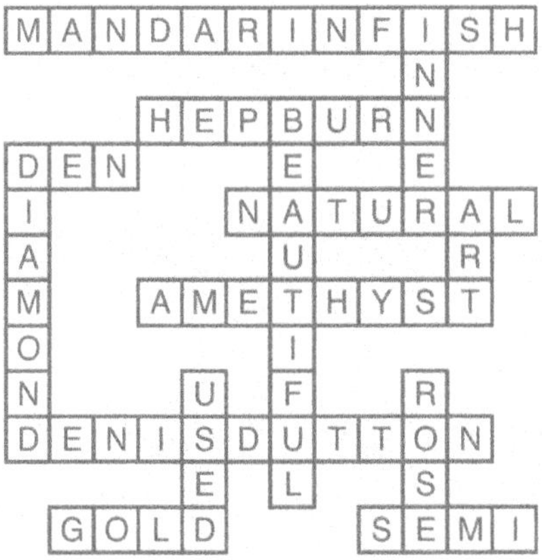

Splurge on Something Special (p. 31)

- **Words:** chocolate truffles, flower bouquet, jewelry, staycation, planned trip, spa appointment, binge show, extra sleep, watch, necklace
- **Answer:** All about luxury

Find Your Flow (p. 33)

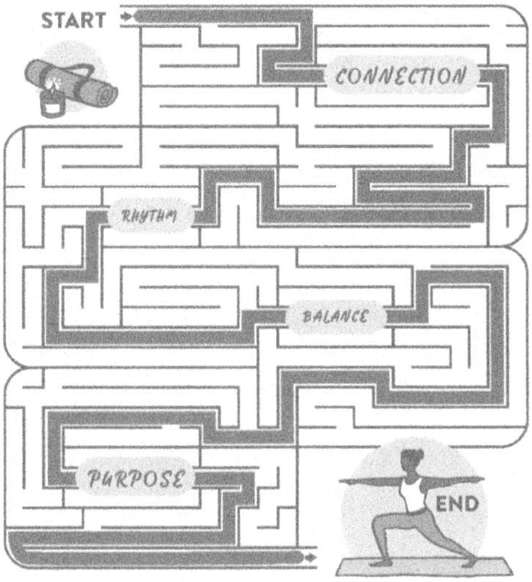

Forgive Yourself (p. 34)

Seek Forgiveness (p. 36)

Find a Path to Success (p. 42)

Track Your Health (p. 37)

- **Words:** mood, nutrition, slumber, workout, positive thoughts, accomplishment, job goals, friendship, lessons learned

- **Answer:** Keep a journal

Celebrate Your Power (p. 44)

- **Words:** resilience, bounce back, survivor, keep going, courage, tough, overcome obstacles, not weak, fighter, muscle power

- **Answer:** True warrior

Think Positively (p. 40)

Find Your Inner Child (p. 45)

Love Your Body Through Nutrition (p. 47)

Embrace Spontaneity (p. 51)

Accept Your Imperfections (p. 49)

Be Brave (p. 55)

Overcome Common Challenges (p. 50)

- **Words:** paranoia, perfectionist, resists change, procrastination, defeatism, rejection, failure, resentment, uncertainty, loneliness

- **Answer:** Life purpose

Radiate Inner Happiness (p. 57)

Enjoy Gentle Touch (p. 59)

- **Words:** praise, kissing, thoughtful, sensual, hold hands, kindly, caressing, warmly, back rub, pleasure, intimacy
- **Answer:** Physical touch

Show Affection (p. 60)

Embrace Life's Adventures (p. 63)

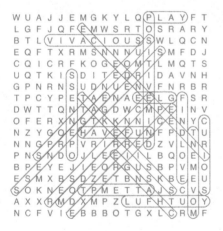

Find Inner Peace (p. 66)

Be Mindful (p. 67)

- **Words:** meditate, yoga practice, calming, tranquility, clear mind, reflection, jot down, breathe, focus, concentration
- **Answer:** Inner peace

Keep Stress Low (p. 73)

Be a Positive Influence (p. 77)

Find Romance (p. 80)

- **Words:** heartfelt, date night, romantic, lovingly, renew vows, diamonds, wooing, embrace, engagement, soulmate
- **Answer:** I love you tons

Trust Your Instincts (p. 82)

Limit Things That Suck Your Energy (p. 85)

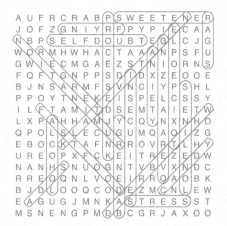

Own Your Worth (p. 90)

Find Your Purpose (p. 92)

- **Words:** inspired, awestruck, lustful, magnetic, breathtaking, forceful, popular, must have, desirable, intrigue
- **Answer:** Positive passion

Find Ways to Recharge (p. 95)

Heal Through Self-Care (p. 103)

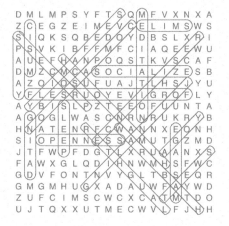

Dream Big (p. 97)

Seize Your Opportunities (p. 105)

Follow Your Wildest Dreams (p. 100)

Show Off Your New Talents (p. 107)